God's Ten Commandments for Kids

Illustrated & Written by

Colleena Roberts

Copyright © 2025 Colleena Roberts
All rights reserved.

No part of this book may be reproduced, stored in a retrieval system, or transmitted in any form or by any means—electronic, mechanical, photocopying, recording, or otherwise—without the prior written permission of the author, except in the case of brief quotations for reviews or educational use.

This book is a work of faith-based literature intended to educate and inspire children about the Ten Commandments. While great care has been taken to ensure biblical accuracy, the author assumes no responsibility for errors or omissions.

Illustrations Generated using AI

Cover Design by Colleena Roberts

Self-Published by Colleena Roberts
Printed in the United States of America

For inquiries, contact: *Colleena.roberts@gmail.com*

Scripture References:

Unless otherwise noted, all Scripture quotations are taken from the New International Version (NIV). The final quote on the closing page is from the King James Version (KJV).

First Edition

Dedication

To my blessed children, *Nina & Jahnoy*

You are my greatest blessing and inspiration. May t[his] book plant seeds of faith in your hearts and guide y[ou] to walk in God's love. Always remember, His wisdo[m] will light your path, and His commandments will ke[ep] you strong. I pray you grow to know Him deeply a[nd] carry His truth with you always.

With all my love,

Mommy

"Train up a child in the way he should go: and when he is old, he will not depart from it."
Proverbs 22:6 (KJV)

First Commandment

Love God First

"You shall have other gods befo[re] Me" –Exodus 20

What does t[his] mean?

God wants to the most important pa[rt] of our lives! H[e] loves us mor[e] than anythin[g] and wants us love Him bac[k]

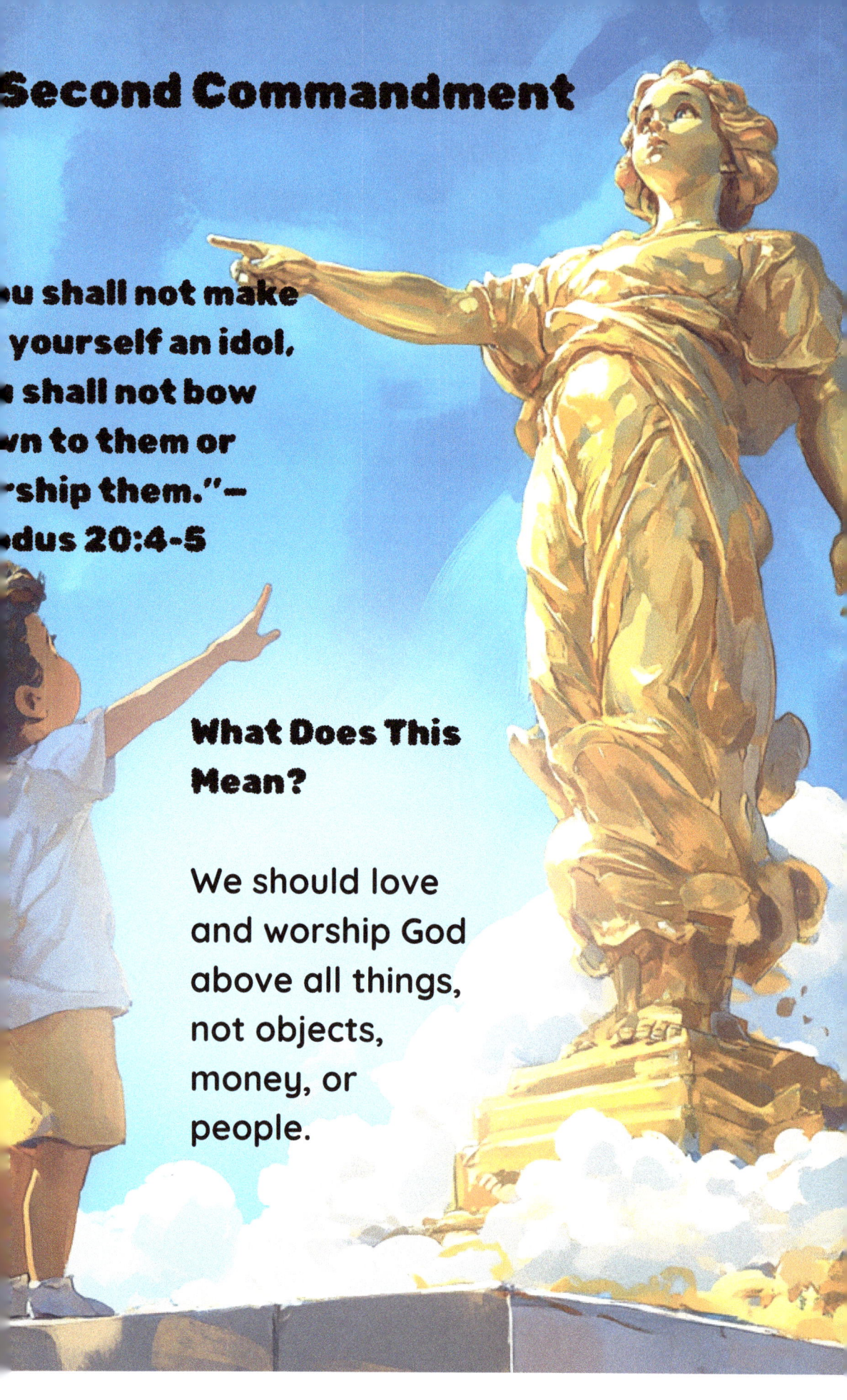

Second Commandment

"You shall not make for yourself an idol, you shall not bow down to them or worship them." – Exodus 20:4-5

What Does This Mean?

We should love and worship God above all things, not objects, money, or people.

Third Commandment

"You shall not misuse the name the Lord your God." – Exodus 2

What does this mean?

God's name is holy and powerful. We should use it with love and respect, not as a joke or when we're angry.

Fourth Commandment

"Remember the Sabbath day, to keep it holy." – Exodus 20:8

What does this mean?

God gave us a special day to rest and spend time with Him. It's a time to pray, be with family, and take a break from work or chores.

Fifth Commandment

"Honor your father and your mother."– (Exodus 20:12)

What This Means:

God wants us to respect and listen to our parents. They help guide us, love us, and teach us right from wrong. Honoring them means being kind, obeying their rules, and showing gratitude for all they do.

Sixth Commandment

"You shall not murder." (Exodus 20:13)

What This Means:

God values every life, and He wants us to treat others with love and kindness. This commandment is not just about harming someone physically but also about our words and actions. When we speak with kindness and forgive others, we choose love over anger.

Seventh Commandmen

"You shall not commit adultery." — (Exodus 20:14)

What This Means:

God teaches us that love is a promise. Marriage is a special bond that should be honored with faithfulness, kindness, and trust. Keeping our promises to one another pleases God and helps build strong, happy families.

Eighth Commandment

"You shall not STEAL." – (Exodus 20:15)

What does this mean?

We should respect what belongs to others and never take anything that isn't ours. Taking things without asking is stealing, and it's not loving or fair.

Ninth Commandment

"You shall not give false testimony against your neighbor." – (Exodus 20:16)

What does this mean?

We should always tell the truth and be honest, because lying hurts others and breaks trust.

Tenth Commandment

What does this mean?

Be happy with what you have because God has already given you wonderful things.

"Do not desire what belongs to someone else— their house, spouse, or anything they have."—Exodus 20:17

A Special Message for You

Thank you for reading The 10 Commandments for Kids! I [hope] this book helps you understand how much God loves you [and] how He wants us to live with kindness, honesty, and lov[e.]

Remember, following God's commandments isn't abo[ut] being perfect—it's about trying our best every day an[d] trusting Him to guide us. Keep learning, keep growing, a[nd] always keep God first!

With love and blessings,
Colleena R.

A Payer for You

Dear God,

Thank You for teaching us Your Ten Commandments. Help us always follow Your ways and make good choices every day. Fill our hearts with kindness, honesty, and love for others. When we make mistakes, remind us that You are always ready to forgive us and guide us back to You.

Bless our families, our friends, and everyone who helps us learn more about You. Let Your light shine in our hearts so that we may grow in wisdom and always do what is right.

In Jesus' name, we pray,

Amen.

Illustrated
by
Steve Thomason

A Cartoonist's Guide to the Gospel of John

Rev. Dr. Steve Thomason, PhD

Published by:

Vibble Books

www.stevethomason.net/books

All rights reserved. No part of this book may be reproduced or transmitted in any form or by any means, electronic or mechanical, including photocopying, recording or by any information storage and retrieval system without written permission from the author.

Scripture quotations are from Common Bible: New Revised Standard Version Bible, copyright © 1989 National Council of the Churches of Christ in the United States of America. Used by permission. All rights reserved worldwide.

Copyright © 2022 Steven P. Thomason

ISBN: 979-8-9862444-0-2
Cover Artwork and Interior Illustration: Steven P. Thomason

Printed in the United States of America

Introduction

About This Book

This book brings together two of my passions. The first is preaching and teaching scripture. The second is art. This graphic novel was originally illustrated as a visual supplement to a sermon series on the Gospel of John that we preached between Christmas 2021 - Easter 2022 in the church I served at that time. The illustrations were used in PowerPoints during the sermons and as handouts for weekly study.

Our preaching team followed the texts determined by The Narrative Lectionary. There were many passages left out of the series due to a limited amount of time and a large amount of scripture. So, I decided to illustrate the entire Gospel, not just the texts selected for preaching.

It was my personal challenge to illustrate all the texts in John that fell between the texts we preached each week. I posted each page online and shared them with my blog followers as soon as they were completed. It was tons of fun to watch the digital graphic novel unfold. You can view the digital version of this book and download the PowerPoints and printable PDF documents at *www.cartoonistbible.com/john*.

Now it is my pleasure to share this piece of art and scripture with you in a printed format. There is something satisfying about holding a book in your hand and soaking in the artwork in real space.

I hope you will enjoy reading this book as much as I did making it.

About the Author

I am a pastor, teacher, and an artist. These three aspects of who I am play together in various ways. I am an associate professor of Spiritual Formation and Discipleship at Luther Seminary where I earned a PhD in Missional Leadership. I am also an ordained pastor in the Evangelical Lutheran Church in America (ELCA) and a freelance illustrator. Nearly every sermon I preach and lesson I teach has some form of cartoon involved to help learners visualize biblical and theological concepts.

I invite you to explore my collection of visual resources around the Bible, Spirituality, Theology and Art at my website:

www.stevethomason.net

John at a Glance

The Gospel of John is unique among the four Gospels. There are two significant differences between John and the Synoptics (Matthew, Mark, Luke):

Geography. Matthew, Mark, and Luke share a similar chrological pattern to Jesus' life. In those stories he spends the first few years of his ministry in Galilee, and then dramatically enters Jerusalem for the last week to face his crucifixion and then is resurrected from the dead. John, however, places Jesus back and forth between Galilee and Jerusalem throughout his ministry.

Style. Matthew, Mark, and Luke emphasize more what Jesus said and did, and let the reader decide who Jesus is. John, however, is very clearly making bold theological statements that Jesus is the Word of God made flesh. This book is a theological biography of Jesus.

Outline

Introduction: Chapter 1

The Gospel begins with a poem that connects Jesus to both Genesis and Exodus. Jesus is the Word of God made flesh that dwells among us. John the Baptist is the witness to show us Jesus' identity.

Book of Signs: Chapters 2-11

Jesus does a series of things that John calls *signs* that point to Jesus' true identity. He turns water to wine, has radical conversations, heals people, feeds thousands, makes bold claims about himself, and raises the dead. All of these things are intended to help you trust that he is who he claims to be.

Final Week: Chapters 12-19

Jesus' signs cause a disruption among the people. Some say he is the Messiah. Some say he's crazy. The religious leaders want to suppress his movement before he evokes the wrath of Rome. Just before he is to be betrayed and executed, Jesus spends five chapters comforting his closest friends and promising that the Holy Spirit would be with them when he is gone.

Resurrection Life: Chapters 20-21

Jesus rises from the dead and appears to Mary Magdalene and the disciples. He breathes the Holy Spirit on them and assures them that they can trust him. Finally, Jesus restores Peter and offers hope to all his disciples that forgiveness and restoration are the resurrection life.

Use the index on the next page to locate each story and chapter of John in the graphic novel. The chapter reference is located in the upper left corner of the section and the corresponding page number is in the lower right corner.

INTRODUCTION

1:1-18 PROLOGUE — PAGE 1	1:19-51 CALLING DISCIPLES — PAGE 2

BOOK OF SIGNS

2:1-25 WATER TO WINE — PAGE 3	3:1-36 NICODEMUS — PAGE 4	4:1-54 WOMAN AT THE WELL — PAGE 5	5:1-47 HEALS ON SABBATH — PAGE 6	6:1-71 FEEDS 5,000 — PAGE 7
7:1-52 LIVING WATER — PAGE 8	8:1-59 LIGHT OF THE WORLD — PAGE 9	9:1-34 HEALS BLIND MAN — PAGE 10	9:35-10:42 GOOD SHEPHERD — PAGE 11	11:1-57 RAISES LAZARUS — PAGE 12

FINAL WEEK

12:1-26 ENTERS JERUSALEM — PAGE 13	THE UPPER ROOM	18:1-11 — PAGE 18	18:12-27 PETER'S DENIAL — PAGE 19
12:27-50 SUMMARY STATEMENTS — PAGE 14	13:1-38 WASHES FEET — PAGE 15	18:28-40 — PAGE 20	19:1-16 TRIAL WITH PILATE — PAGE 21
	14-15 WORDS OF COMFORT — PAGE 16	19:17-42 CRUCIFIXION — PAGE 22	
	16-17 PRAYER FOR UNITY — PAGE 17		

RESURRECTION LIFE

20:1-18 APPEARS TO MARY — PAGE 23	20:19-31 ASSURES THOMAS — PAGE 24	21:1-24 RESTORES PETER — PAGE 25

iii

The Political Landscape of Jesus' World

Jesus did not live in a vacuum. He was a real person who lived in a real time and place with real social and political issues buzzing in the air. He was a Jewish man living in Galilee during the first century. The Roman Empire had conquered the land and was an occupying, oppressive presence in every part of the country.

The Jewish people believed that they were the chosen people of the one true God, Yahweh. God had promised their ancestor, Abraham, that he would become a great nation and be a blessing to all nations.

"How long would God allow the Romans to occupy their land?"

"When would the Messiah come and deliver them to restore God's Kingdom?"

These were the questions that undoubtedly lurked in every Jew's mind while Jesus walked the earth.

It is important to note that there was not one type of Jew in Jesus' day any more than there is one type of Christian in our day. There were at least five distinct sects of Judaism when Jesus lived.

> **The Herodians** were Jews who recognized the power of the Roman Empire and bowed to it. These Jews, led by King Herod, adopted Graeco-Roman culture and introduced it to Israel. For example, Herod built Roman circuses (horse racing stadiums) and theaters in Israel.
>
> **The Sadducees** were the aristocracy of Israel. They were wealthy land owners who were tied to the Priestly tribes and the sacrificial rituals associated with the Temple.
>
> **The Pharisees** were teachers and strict followers of the Law of Moses. They represented the working class of Israel and desired to purify the nation of all foreign influence.
>
> **The Zealots** were political revolutionaries who sought to overthrow Rome through violent uprising.
>
> **The Essenes** were scholars and monks who chose to remove themselves from society and seek God in the wilderness.

These five groups vied for power and influence in Israel during Jesus' life. Ultimately, all but the Pharisees were destroyed in A.D. 70.

Notice how Jesus interacts with the various religious leaders as you read through the Gospel of John.

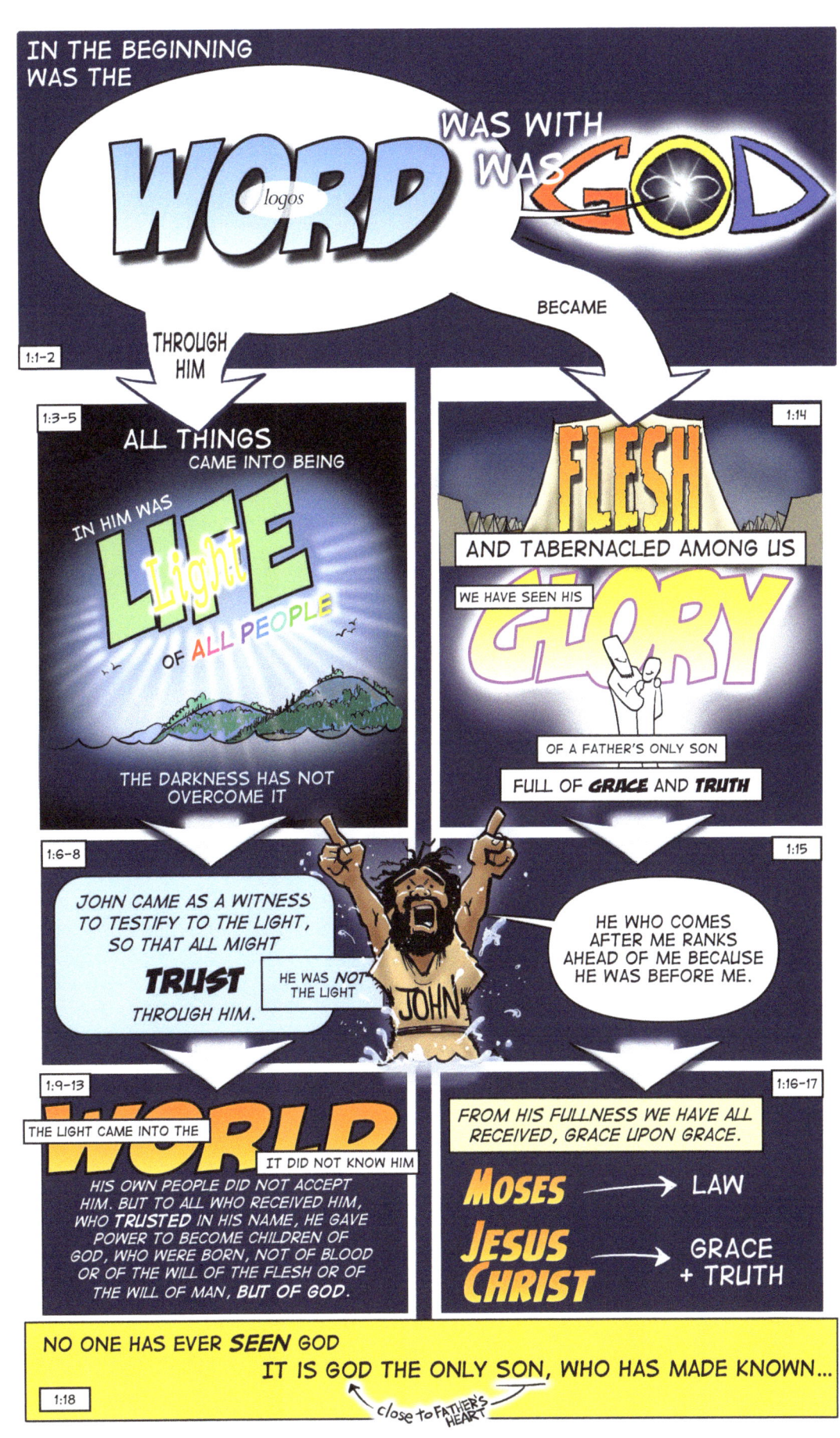

FESTIVAL OF TABERNACLES

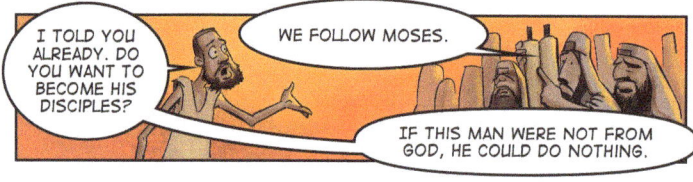

FESTIVAL OF THE DEDICATION

BEFORE THE PASSOVER FESTIVAL

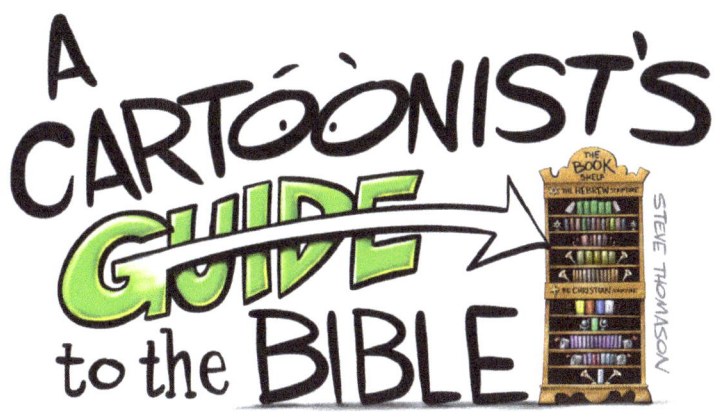

Fun pictures. Serious study.

Explore the Bible through engaging, whimsical illustrations and compelling Biblical scholarship. A Cartoonist's Guide to the Bible offers:

- free online visual commentaries of the Bible,
- downloads of PowerPoints and images that you can use in your own preaching and teaching,
- printable PDF documents to use as handouts,
- links to other helpful online resources for Bible study,
- an online community to connect with other Bible students, teachers, and preachers.

www.cartoonistbible.com

www.ingramcontent.com/pod-product-compliance
Ingram Content Group UK Ltd.
Pitfield, Milton Keynes, MK11 3LW, UK
UKHW060217240426
12048UKWH00030BB/1701